The Usborne
Pirates
Coloring
and Activity
Book

Designed and illustrated by

Candice "Quickdraw" Whatmore

Written by

Kirsteen "Razor-quill" Robson

Pirates consultant:
Tony "Blizzard Whiskers" Pawlyn

Who's who in a pirate crew

Pirates were ruthless robbers who roamed the salty seas in search of ships or vulnerable seaside villages to steal from. Far from being a lazy, lawless lot, pirates had to work as a disciplined team, and most men had particular jobs to do to keep the vessel shipshape and the crew alive.

Here are descriptions of a few important characters on board a pirate ship. Can you match them to the correct pictures?

1. The captain was voted into the job by his men. He was expected to be a skilled sailor and a bold leader in battle.

2. The quartermaster was second in command. He shared out food, gunpowder, loot, work and punishment.

3. The ship's carpenter was responsible for mending the ship – filling in the holes and keeping it seaworthy.

A

B

C

D

E

F

4. Rats and mice ran riot on ships, so a canny crew often carried a cat to keep these rodent rascals under control.

5. The cabin boy was learning the pirate trade. He often ran errands for the captain, and laid out his clothes.

6. Fortunate crews had a surgeon to treat their injuries. Less lucky shipmates had to make do with anyone who could brandish a blade.

The Jolly Roger

No pirate ship was complete without a "Jolly Roger" – a fearsome flag displaying a doom-laden design that would strike terror into the heart of anyone who saw it. A skull and crossbones was a popular emblem, but anything would do as long as its message was clear and threatening.

Create your own bloodcurdling Jolly Roger design.

These pictures show some popular alternatives to the traditional skull-and-crossbones emblem.

Pirate provisions

Before setting sail, pirates needed to stock up on supplies. The list below includes some of the things they would need to take with them to sea. (The pictures on the right include some more lighthearted suggestions.)

See if you can find the words below in the grid. They may be written in any direction. Starting at the top, read the unused letters to spell the first lines of a pirate song from a famous pirate story.

```
S S A P M O C H A R T S F
P I F T B E E R E E N M E
Y N S E L P P A F O N T S
G U N P O W D E R H E D E
L S R T A E M D E K O M S
A A E E A D P I S T O L S
S I T M A N S C H H E S A
S L N T Y O H O W H O A L
N C A N N O N B A L L S T
D L L A H A R D T A C K U
J O L L Y R O G E R B O C
T T I T L E O F R O P E S
R H O U M M E D I C I N E
```

APPLES • BEER • CANNONBALLS • CHARTS • COMPASS • CUTLASSES
FRESH WATER • GUNPOWDER • HARD TACK • JOLLY ROGER • MEDICINE
OIL LANTERNS • PISTOLS • ROPES • SAILCLOTH • SMOKED MEAT • SPY GLASS

_ _

_ _

5 PIECES

Pirate Store

OPEN TO PAYING PIRATES ONLY

PARROTS
HALF-PRICE OFFER

APOTHECARY

WOODEN EYEBALLS

SCURVY TONIC

LEECHES
Cures: Gangrene, Scurvy, Pink Eye and much more

SEA SALT FOR WOUNDS

ALL HOOKS

Made to measure while you wait

CHARTS

TRIED AND TESTED

FREE ENGRAVING ON ALL TANKARDS

KEEP CALM AND DRINK RUM

I ♥ THE CARIBBEAN

PIRATES RULE YO HO!

LUXURY HATS 2 PIECES

EYE PATCHES AND HEAD SCARVES

Choose from our latest designs (SPOTS OR STRIPES)

TREASURE CHESTS – STARTER to LARGE

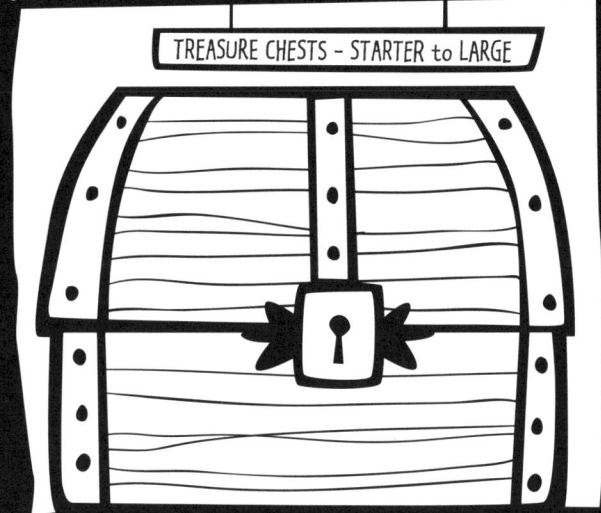

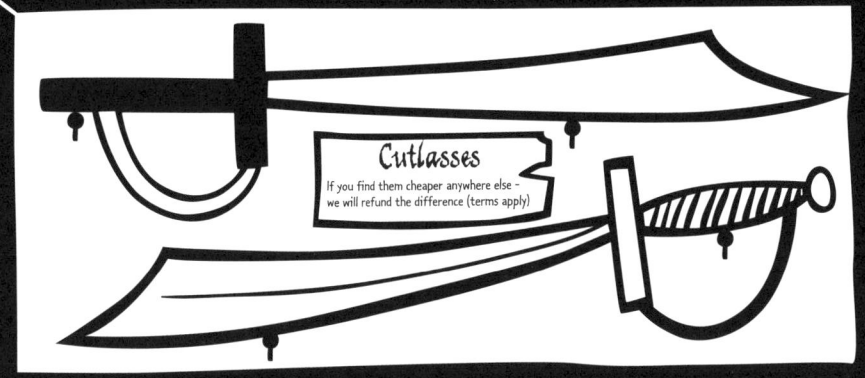

Cutlasses

If you find them cheaper anywhere else – we will refund the difference (terms apply)

Mealtime misery

It was incredibly difficult to keep food fresh for long during a voyage, so mealtimes often caused pirates more dread than delight. Here you can find out about some of the foods a pirate might find on his plate.

Show how many eggs Clucky has laid this week.

At the start of a voyage pirates ate fresh meat, cheese, vegetables and eggs. Livestock such as hens and cows lived on board for as long as they could be fed, then they were eaten.

Doodle in the basket to show what the pirates have caught in their nets.

Pirates might catch fresh fish or turtles at sea to add variety to their diet.

Draw another barrel of salted meat.

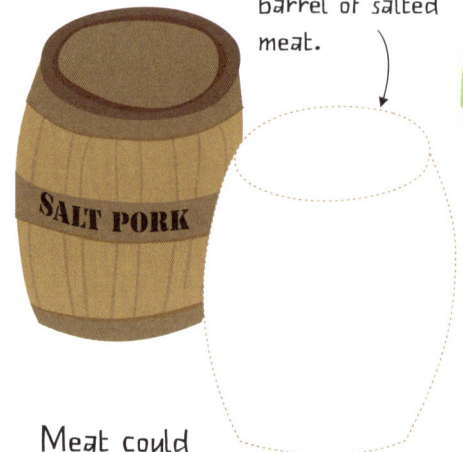

SALT PORK

Meat could be preserved by salting or smoking it and sealing it in barrels. Meat preserved in this way was tough and chewy.

What's he thinking?

In 1670, the starving pirate crew of Sir Henry Morgan sliced up their leather satchels, roasted them and ate them.

Add more weevils to the hard tack.

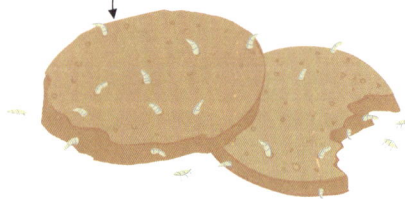

Hard tack - dry bread made of flour and water. Pirates often ate it in the dark so they couldn't see the weevils that had infested them.

Fill in the flasks to show what this pirate is drinking today.

Water soon went stale in its dusty barrels, so pirates often drank beer or rum. If this ran out, they might have to drink salty seawater or even their own urine.

Rules and punishments

Although pirates lived outside the law of the land, they had their own strict code of conduct. There were unpleasant punishments for anyone found flouting the rules.

Popular pirate punishments included:
- being tied to a mast and whipped with a frayed rope called a cat-o'-nine-tails
- being towed behind the boat in the freezing water for a day or two
- being marooned (left alone on a desert island)

If you were a pirate captain, what rules would you add to the list (if your crew agreed) and what would be the punishment for breaking them?

Pirate rules

1. Equal vote for all
2. No stealing from shipmates
3. No gambling on board
4. Lights out at 8 o'clock
5. Keep your weapons clean
6. No women on board
7. No deserting – stick together
8. No fighting shipmates at sea
9. Treasure shared fairly according to rank
10. Musicians have Sundays off

Rule	Punishment

After eight

Lights out was at 8 o'clock sharp. While the captain curled up in a comfortable bed in his private cabin, the rest of the crew hauled themselves into grubby hammocks in the belly of the ship. There in the stuffy darkness, amid hissing cockroaches and the scratching of scrounging rats, they were rocked to sleep by the rhythm of the restless waves.

Show whether this slumbering sailor is snarling or smiling, and draw his dream.

Ship ahoy!

On spying a merchant ship crossing their path, pirates had two choices. They could take down their Jolly Roger and hoist a normal flag instead to let the other ship think it was safe to get close (until it was too late). Or they could make themselves look as menacing and merciless as possible to fill their enemies with tummy-trembling terror.

If the pirates had already captured a few ships, they might raise a pirate flag on each of them to look like a whole fleet of pirate vessels. Add more flags, masts and sails to the boats below.

Moonlight marauders

Thinking the merchant sailors are sweetly slumbering, these bold buccaneers have swarmed aboard with bloodcurdling bellows. But a swift and sinister hiss of steel tells them that their opponents have been waiting watchfully for them, and a bloody battle begins...

Read about some of the weapons that might be used in a raid.

Daggers were handy knives for hiding in pockets to whip out and surprise enemies.

Cutlasses were short, sharp slashing swords, often with a cupped or basket-shaped hand guard.

Spiked iron caltrops (or crowsfeet) were scattered on deck, ready to pierce the (often bare) feet of unsuspecting sailors.

Pistols were fine for flooring foes from afar, but they were awkward to aim accurately on choppy seas. (Damp gunpowder didn't fire well either, and it took ages to reload them.)

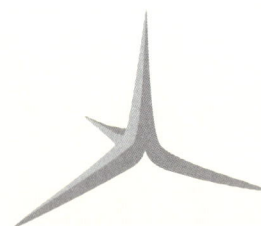

Grappling hooks could be thrown into the rigging, or over the side of another ship, to drag it close enough to jump aboard.

Grenadoes were gunpowder-filled throwing balls of iron or wood that exploded when the fuse was lit.

Sometimes pirates added tar and rags to the grenado mixture, creating choking clouds of black smoke to cause confusion.

Myths and mistakes

Pirates have captured the imagination of so many storytellers and movie-makers that all kinds of fables are now thought of as facts. For instance, some pirates may have lost a leg or an eye, but a ship couldn't sail without plenty of able-bodied crewmen. And few real pirates would bother to make their prisoners walk the plank – they'd just push them overboard.

How to draw a storybook pirate captain

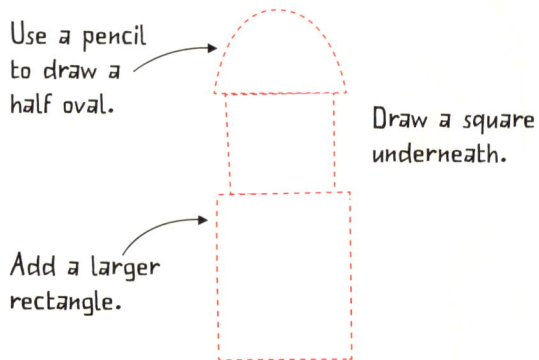

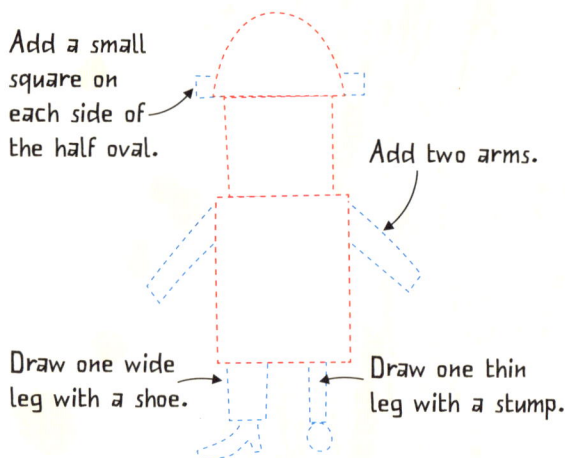

Use a pencil to draw a half oval.

Draw a square underneath.

Add a larger rectangle.

Add a small square on each side of the half oval.

Add two arms.

Draw one wide leg with a shoe.

Draw one thin leg with a stump.

Draw a face, eye patch and bushy beard.

Use a pen to draw around the outline and fill in the hat and beard.

Add a hand to one arm and a hook to the other.

Add details such as a shirt, belt and jacket.

Pirate pastimes

Aside from surviving sea battles and storms, much of a pirate's time was spent keeping the ship seaworthy – patching sails, splicing (joining) ropes and making sure the woodwork was watertight. Once their jobs were done, nothing could beat singing a few swinging sea shanties to keep boredom at bay, or sneaking a few forbidden games of cards or dice.

Finish the pirate faces.

The truth about treasure

After a successful skirmish, a lucky looter might find a stash of coins or jewels, but fresh food and medicine were rich rewards too. People could also be priceless prizes – think how popular a pirate would be with his wounded shipmates if he brought a super-skilled surgeon back on board.

When it came to dividing the booty, pirates were usually fair fellows and took (more or less) equal shares. Use the clues below to find out who took each piece of treasure from their latest conquest.

o Captain Grizzlebeard's treasure isn't silver.

o Mumbles McGraw can't use his treasure at the table.

o The ugliest pirate has the most delicate and decorative prize.

Spanish gold doubloons – each one was worth about a week's wages for an ordinary pirate.

Silverware

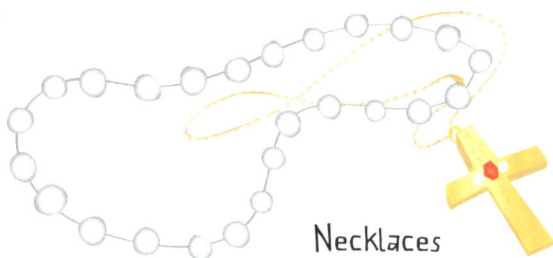

Necklaces

Pieces of eight were silver coins made in Spain.

Captain Grizzlebeard

Mumbles McGraw

Scurvy Joe Jones

Scarface Jake

Treasure map

In real life, pirates would usually trade or gamble with their share of a treasure haul, or take it home. If they *did* decide to hide it for safekeeping, a map was probably the worst way to keep their secret safe. But this has not stopped treasure maps from playing an important part in many pirate tales.

These instructions describe two routes to some buried treasure. Captain Crossbones took the first route and Captain Cutthroat followed the second. Who reached the treasure first?

From the pointed pair on the island of mud, head west to the isle of fiery rock. Sail south to the place where the dolphins dive then travel eastward until a monster blocks thy path. Steer to the south then drop anchor and trek to the mountains of mist and shadow. Wend thy way between the three and the one then seek the swirling plain of shifting sands. Head southwest and dig under the lonely pine tree for thy prize.

Set sail south of the twin palms on the isle of mud. Steer southwesterly past the diving dolphins and through the narrow pass. Follow the coast but be sure to sail between the pointed peaks or scuttled will ye surely be. Skirt around the Pointing Peninsula, turn northeast and drop anchor in the bay. Head east and delve deep at the foot of the lonesome pine tree for thy reward.

TREASURE MAP

Smugglers' Cove

Twin Peaks

Buccaneer Bay

Lava Island

Swamp Island

Silver Sands Bay

Grim Gulf

Serpent Seas

Dire Straits

Murky Mountains

Rugged Rocks

Dead Man's Cavern

Treasure Island

Quicksand Plains

N
NW   NE
W   E
SW   SE
S

Thar She Blows!

Pointing Peninsula

Cape of No Hope

Offshore dangers

Out at sea, wild winds could whip the waters into a frenzy, sinking the sturdiest of ships. Or smothering fogs could force ships to sail blind until they were lost beyond hope or ruined on the razor-toothed rocks. And as if these terrors weren't enough, seafarers shared superstitious tales of vast sea monsters with thrashing tentacles that brought doom and destruction.

Help the ship to avoid the obstacles and navigate its way safely to the sandy island.

The perils of piracy

Pirates' lives were often short. Shipwreck, starvation or sickness sent many sailors straight to Davy Jones' Locker (that's pirate-speak for the seabed.) Cannon fire or combat ended plenty of promising pirate careers while some sea dogs were captured by the navy and hanged for their crimes. Only the luckiest old salts survived to enjoy their pirated plunder into retirement.

You could use this space to write your own tale of pirate adventure.

"Ahoy there!" shouted Captain . . . .

"Where can I find . . . .

. . . .

. . . .

. . . .

. . . .

. . . .

. . . .

. . . .

The end

Rogues' Gallery

Some pirates became famous as tales of their treachery spread far and wide. Over time, their dreadful deeds inspired writers to spin stories about pirate characters of their own. On the opposite page you can find out more about a few of the most famous fiends of fact and fiction.

Why not draw your own pirate character, and give him a name.

WANTED!
FOR PIRACY AND LOOTING

LONG JOHN SILVER

Long John Silver was a fictional pirate from the book 'Treasure Island' by Robert Louis Stevenson. Silver's left leg had been cut off at the hip after a sea battle, but he hopped around very nimbly using a crutch. He had a parrot companion named Captain Flint who sat on his shoulder. In the book Silver and his shipmates trick their way onto an expedition in search of buried treasure.

Henry Morgan

Henry Morgan was a privateer which meant he had permission from the government to raid foreign ships. He became one of the richest pirates ever.

Black Bart

Nicknamed Black Bart, Bartholomew Roberts was a daredevil pirate famous for attacking ships that had more cannons than his. Unusually for a pirate, he was well known for preferring a tankard of tea to a tot of rum. He gained the reputation for being invincible – until his death four years into his pirate career.

BLACKBEARD

Blackbeard's real (but less terrifying) name was Edward Teach. To boost his already alarming image, he sometimes tucked burning ropes under his hat, cloaking himself in clouds of smoke.

Captain Hook

Captain James Hook is a character in J.M. Barrie's book 'Peter Pan.' The pirate's name refers to the large metal hook he wore in place of his right hand, which Peter Pan had cut off and fed to a crocodile. The croc liked the taste so much it followed Hook around, hoping to finish its meal.

MARY READ AND ANN BONNY

Women were strictly forbidden on pirate ships, so female pirates were rare. Mary Read and Ann Bonny disguised themselves as men and joined the pirate crew of a captain named Calico Jack. They fought even more fiercely than their male shipmates.

Coloring hints and tips

Use felt-tip pens or colored pencils to color in the pictures. Felt-tip pens will give you strong colors, while pencils will have a softer effect.

You can draw patterns within some of the shapes. For example, this scene is decorated with spots and dots...

...waves and wiggles...

...stripes.

You could finish this picture to practice coloring.

Fill in larger areas such as this island with lots of lines going in the same direction.

It's a good idea to lay your book on a flat surface while you are coloring, or slip a piece of cardboard under the page you are filling in, to make a firm surface.

If you want to cut out your picture, you'll find a dotted line on each page to cut along.